From Doormat to Diva

Taking Center Stage in Your Own Life

Ten Steps to Personal Stardom

ISBN 1-58961-145-4

Published by PageFree Publishing, Inc.
733 Howard Street
Otsego, Michigan 49078
616-692-3386
www.pagefreepublishing.com

From Doormat to Diva

Taking Center Stage in Your Own Life

Ten Steps to Personal Stardom

by

MERCI MIGLINO

Acknowledgements

Thank you to: My family for believing in me despite the unpredictability of this *Diva* adventure. The Blessed Virgin Mother for her constant care, for being one of the greatest Divas of all-time (just think Wedding at Cana when she ordered the son of God to make more wine!) and who is always by my side. My grandmother for giving me my first taste of Diva-ness at such an early age. Barbara Wisnom for her wonderful workshop, From Princess to Queen", the inspiration for my title. Linda Carter for helping me to see that I am creative, resourceful and whole. Mary Lee Miglino for her fierce support and encouragement. Ray Patterson for seeing my value so clearly. Judith Garten, for being my 50-50 Pathwork Helper and giving form to many of the life lessons I bring to this book. Donna Gadomski for her warm hospitality and kick-ass proofreading skills that allowed me to finish this book in record time. Pat Sears Doherty who edited this book and who showed me that seemingly ordinary people have extraordinary things to say. To all my clients, past and present, who inspired me and gave me the opportunity to express my wisdom and to integrate their wisdom into mine.

The whimsical and clever cartoon of yours truly found on the cover of this book is the creative interpretation of me, the Delightful Diva, by Randy Rumpf, artist and owner of Design Works in Troy, NY. Thanks, Randy, for 'getting' what this book is all about even though you are not a Diva in the true sense of the word, you are indeed divinely talented and a joy to work with.

This book is an accumulation of a lifetime of learning, of all the influences in my life –from the Catholic Church to the 50-50 Pathwork training from the great fiction classics to the millions of self-help books I devoured over the years, from the Twelve Steps to the musical spirit of reggae, pop, rock and new age, from my therapists to my grandmothers, from my experiences in politics to commission jewelry sales, from the great and near-great people I have met and those whose greatness is yet to be discovered.

Table of Contents

When I was a child, I always thought the world was mine,
A stomping ground for me, full of opportunities. I always had
this attitude that I was going to go out into the world and do all
the things I wanted to do."
- Madonna

"I have the stardom glow"
- Jennifer Lopez

Intro

So, what happened to the diva in me? What happened to the girl who was convinced of her own choices, bold enough to use her imagination, and powerful enough to get others to go along with her energy and enthusiasm?

The world got a hold of me, that's what. And before I knew it, it was all about fitting in, making myself small so others wouldn't feel uncomfortable, rolling up my boldness in favor of security, or what I thought was security. In short, I made a trade off. Dimming my unique and inner light so I wouldn't outshine others…

In childhood we are often more spirit, more divine, than human. We have not been 'of the world' for so long that we lose all hope – even those of us born into a less than functional family. Like most struggling divas we lost sight of this child…this divine spirit that has yet to be fully expressed.

As a 9-year old, I wrote poetry and short stories. I spent hours daydreaming of being the next Lois Lane, a reporter for a 'large metropolitan newspaper.' I secretly wanted to act, to be onstage, to be the center of attention. But in my childish view I could not see how this was even remotely possible. I did not have a vision. Nor the resources and support needed. So I somehow connected wanting 'center stage' with a lonely and hard life. There is no blame or regret here. I have come to understand that these trials, these obstacles and challenges were the road I needed to travel to get where I am right now. Right here.

Every experience I had – and there are quite a few – became a tool in my box to use at the proper time. I grew up adept at peacekeeping in my family. I knew at an early age how to motivate and enthuse people into doing things – even things they did not want to do. I used humor to make myself attractive, to make up for a chubby body. I loved, loved, loved anything to do with cosmetics – and would have become a hairdresser had my mother not put her foot down and enrolled me in a community college. I did, however, work in salons, learning to sculpt nails as well as the pure joy of making someone's feet beautiful.

I came out of college a teacher, never really taught in a conventional sense and, yet, I have never stopped teaching. I played around with the graphic arts - proofreading ads for a free weekly advertiser. This led to a job writing articles for the same publication - no 'large metropolitan newspaper' but close enough to qualify as a dream come true. Struck by a sudden need to find a secure career, I completed a certification as a paralegal - working on Wall Street for six months before deciding the law and I was a match made in hell.

So where to next? I began a career in the New York State

Legislature, which lasted 18 years. I wrote for representatives on every subject imaginable. I led teams of writers and researchers. I ran political campaigns – as close to show business as I ever thought I'd get! I eventually managed hundreds of people, saw most every county in the state and served as Director of Communications for, at one time or another, both houses of the Legislature. I was making more money than I thought possible and I was slowly dying.

I had daily migraines, stomach problems, chest pains and a knocked-on-my-ass chronic fatigue. Somewhere in my head I knew the choice was coming down to: "Your money or your life." For a longtime I chose the money even while my body – refusing to cooperate - was thankfully choosing life. Against this backdrop my husband, my rock of Gibraltar, the *Steady Eddie* of my life had an accident on-the-job that violently interrupted our finely honed household balancing act. We are indeed blessed as he is now fully recovered. But during the weeks he recuperated, it changed everything. Just days after he returned home in a back brace, a metal plate in his chin and a jumble of wires around his jaw, he looked at me and said, "If this is what it takes to see that my daughter has a college education then it was worth every bit of it."

No, I did not leave my job there and then. But it was the beginning of a whole new approach to my life. With the help of what I lovingly call the "God Squad" - my sister (a definite Diva!), her husband and their friend - I walked out of the 2000 National Democratic Convention in Los Angeles and in doing so moved... From Doormat to Diva©. Finally I was taking center stage in my own life.

So, no matter how significant the troubles in our lives, whether it's a life-altering event such as illness or accident, an unending list of chores or the problems of money and security, we have what it takes to change our lives. We have all the tools and experiences needed to get where we want to be – to be our own kind of Diva. The following ten steps to personal stardom prepare you for your own Diva-morphsis.

It takes some doing, some real work but I am more times than not the DIVA, that human woman armed with her divine self, and energized by the playful child who sees what she wants and goes after it!

Just like Madonna, Barbra, Oprah and Whitney!

Oh, but I can hear the resistance from here! You are not anything like these women! And you certainly don't want the bad rep of being considered bitchy, self-focused or, God forbid, difficult!

I challenge you to take another look at these women and any women you deem a *Diva*. Are they confident rather than bitchy? Do you know what amplifies their greatness and what doesn't? So what if they are self-directed and deliberate, not easily convinced they must adjust this greatness to appeal to the masses? Do they refuse to make themselves and their talent small? Instead of difficult, could they be simply in charge of their own lives and their talent? Have they figured out that they are the only and final authority on what makes them great?

YES, my divine sisters! And you too can also get there with a little change in perspective! Simple yes. Easy no. Worth your life's energy? YOU BET!

Streisand, Madonna, Whitney and Reba are examples of great singers with personality and talent who have achieved a degree of fame few others have and a legacy based on their achievements.

These are women who have successfully merged selfishness with power, who found center stage despite the challenges of life. Divas! In the pages that follow I give you the 10 steps needed for you (yes you!) to make this transformation! With humor laced with truth I lay out the steps that can move you to the center of your life…no matter what or where your stage may be.

What do I mean by Diva?

The word *diva* is Italian, literally meaning goddess. Its origins are Latin, from the feminine of *divus;* divine, relating to god or spirit. It was first commonly used to describe an operatic prima donna, the leading female soloist in an opera company where, of course, it is also came to describe a temperamental and conceited person.

So what do I mean when I say that I am a *diva*? Everyone is divine and, since we are women we are, in the languages of Italian and Latin, Diva's. We are divine beings, god-like and as creative as our creator her/himself. If we consider that we are made in a likeness of the divine or spirit, in the image of the divine with all its resourcefulness and wholeness, then we can see ourselves as divine beings having a human experience and NOT the other way around.

Now armed with this divinity, the challenge of our earthly lives takes on a whole new meaning. For it is through our humanity that we discover just how divine we are! It is through our pain, hurt, joy and triumph that we truly step into our divinity. In short, it is through the doormat experience that we see the limits of our humanness and begin to tap into the diva within. These holy and spiritual assets have always been there but we have to get to a crisis of sorts, when the tool-of-choice, our tremendous and incredible *will*, is not enough to bring about the change we crave.

When sheer willpower can no longer bring us the desired joy, happiness, fulfillment, we come to a kind of surrender, a laying down of our *will* for a moment – the *will* being our tool of choice in solving our problems. You know, *let's DO something about this! Now!* That's your *will* tool.

Instead we are willing to search within for what is missing, for our dormant and dusty Divinity Tool. Then we understand there is a critical and precarious balance involving both these tools – our divinity and our will - that is essential to manifesting true serenity on earth. And that this serenity is not based on the unrealistic expectation of being perfect or having a perfect, pain free life.

Now disappointments, pain, setbacks, even crises take on new meaning. Rather than obstacles to the life we want, we begin to see them as stepping stones, lessons learned more quickly and with less resistance that can catapult us into Diva-dom.

Now let's begin the diva-morphsis we have always known is possible!

Doormat or DIVA?

Take My Test Below and Find Out!

1. Your boyfriend/husband/partner claims he has too much work to do and cancels your vacation to the Bahamas for the third time. You:

    a. Grab the tickets, call a girlfriend and head for the airport. You'll have a great time!

    b. Stay home and sulk… secretly plotting ways to torture your man – tampering with his morning coffee, putting gum on the bottom of every pair of shoes he owns, calling into his job with a bomb threat – you get the picture…

    c. Feel bad for him and assure him there will always be other trips to the Bahamas.

2. Your best friend just can't get enough of you but frankly you are pooped. She's fun and all but you just can't deal with another night of her. You:

    a. Go into hiding. Shut off all the lights in the house and pretend to be out if she calls or shows up.

    b. Agree to hook up with her. She's not that bad. After all she did sit with you when you had that bad haircut and said you were as cute as a chipmunk. You'll get sleep another time.

c. Tell her you are wiped out. You love her but need your beauty rest. You'll call her when the bags under your eyes are packed and off your face!

3. You are quite happy with your facial features, but lately your nose has been getting you down. What do you do?
a. Start saving for a rhinoplasty immediately!
b. Explore new make-up techniques to play down and compliment your nose.
c. Go with the flow. You decide to get a nose piercing!

4. You are beginning to hate your job and you can't look at your boss without wondering if there is such a thing as a perfect crime. You:
a. Complain to anyone who'll listen and try to look for work but there really isn't anything out there and, besides, you don't know what you really want to do so you might as well take the money.
b. Decide to keep the paycheck and spend time figuring out what's right about the job and what's not…then you sock away the money so you can start that organic edible underwear business you always wanted.
c. Jump out the first open window and into another job lickety split quick.

5. You just won the lottery! You:
a. Head for the travel agency and book a world tour of all 199 countries. FIRST CLASS.
b. You drive straight to a financial planner and make well-

thought-out and careful choices about your future.

c. Jump up and down and say, "Great! Now I can create my dreams and help others create theirs as well."

6. How long does it usually take you to get ready in the morning?

a. Over an hour. You groom yourself like a beauty queen and love every minute of it.

b. Less than 20 minutes. You throw on whatever's handy and say "who cares?" when you look in the mirror.

c. Roughly two hours since you must take care of every member of the household before stealing 10 minutes for yourself.

7. How many things are you tolerating in your life right now?

a. Well, let's see there's the job I could do without, the house is a mess, the kids are driving me crazy and my car is like a landfill on wheels and my mother…don't get me started on my mother…

b. I am not really tolerating anything. I just ignore what isn't right in my life. No use expecting more than I deserve.

c. Not a thing.

8. A friend thinks your name just doesn't have "star" quality. What do you do about it?

a. Nothing, it's only a name. You want to be remembered for being an awesome person, not how cool your name is.

b. Decide to go by your first name only…like Cher or Madonna or Merci.

c. Change it! You can think of plenty more interesting names, anyway.

9. Would you consider yourself a success?

    a. Never. There's always room for improvement.

    b. Not until you're rich and famous!

    c. YES. You are already working toward your dreams and this will make you enough money to live comfortably doing something you love.

10. What expression best represents your attitude toward life?

    a. Whatever…

    b. Divine!

    c. YES!

How much diva support and training do you need?

Scoring –Give yourself 10 points for every right answer. NOTE: Some answers get you partial credit.

1.	a	
2.	c	
3.	c	5pts for b
4.	b	
5.	c	
6.	a	
7.	c	
8.	b	5pts for c
9.	c	
10.	c	5pts for b

100-115 You go girl! You are a total Diva! Hear you roar! You like yourself, your ambitions and your life.

80-99 Yes, you are on your way! A little more training and you will give up those energy-zapping friends, or lose that toxic job. There is so much in store for you! Don't give up!

65-79 You aren't failing at life… but you are in danger of it. You need some remedial help to remind you that what you want, wants you. Find some time and focus on what you want – get a massage to help the process. Stay close, my Diva sister, we will get you through with flying colors.

Below 64 Time for emergency Diva treatment! You might need a weekend of intense self-care, extreme pampering and a perspective makeover. Don't worry, we've seen worse cases come back to live a divinely delightful life! But make no doubt about it - prayer is needed now.

When onstage, I always try to take my audience through as many emotions as I possibly can. I want them to go from laughter to tears, be shocked and surprised and walk out the door with a renewed sense of themselves —
and maybe a smile.
- Reba McEntire

Step 1
Get a Perspective
Makeover!

No, I don't mean a literal makeover. I mean get rid of that drab black and white, all-or-nothing thinking you wrap yourself in every day. Hit the stage with a new and colorful perspective! We need to fully awaken the child within us but with our adult sense of perspective.

When we were children, the world was very much a black and white place. Mom is home, life is good. Mom is away, life is bad. I didn't get that cookie, I am going to die! I get the doll or truck I want, I live!

As adults, we gradually learn that life is not black and white, good or bad. However, while intellectually we may know life is all about the gray between, we hang on to the simplicity of our childhood thinking. And when good or bad things happen, we still may react in black and white terms, as if things are our entire fault or not our fault at all. But life is all the colors between black and white - even, gray.

Once you fully accept, with all your being, that life is not about achieving a perfect, pain-free existence (this is impossible) then you can accept life for the mystery and magic of it. Delight in the fact that we do not know what will happen! Don't look for pain, but when it comes, understand that it is the *resistance* to pain, to the reality of pain as a part of life on earth that you can change! And accept that into every life comes rain! Sometimes a little, sometimes a lot. And when a lot comes, take the fast track to your divinity – your true diva self.

To get to true Diva status at the center of your life…be a colorful character! Color can sway thinking, change actions, and cause reactions. For between black and white lies a spectrum of colorful thought, offering us a rainbow of possibilities for a full and joyful life.

Give up your black and white thinking and put more color in your life!

1. Be passionate. Be red!
Express red with all its vibrancy and loudness. Feel the red of your anger, then let it go... for red is also the color of passion - the flip side of anger. If you rule out red-anger, you rule out red-passion.

2. Embrace the warmth of an orange hearth fire.
This color is about approachability - be open to the warmth that comes your way even when the world feels cold and unwelcoming. There is always a bit of orange-warmth for comfort.

3. Color yourself yellow, the color of optimism.

When you are stuck in that all or nothing thinking, find some yellow, some sunshine in your world. What's good, bright, and possible? Yellow, like the sun, is an upbeat reminder that the climate of our lives changes every day.

4. Take a walk in the green of the forest.

Green suggests stability, restfulness, naturalness– a good place to drop into yourself and listen to the full range of your thoughts – not just the *always* and *never* thoughts that stay on the top of our minds. There's a balanced life in the green.

5. Let the sky blue color of divinity be your refuge.

When facing what feels like (but rarely is) a life-or-death decision – to change jobs, stay in a relationship, let go of an expectation - wrap yourself in the all-knowing blue of spirit. For spirit guides us through all the blues - the sad blues and the calm, peaceful blues of surrendering to our own divinity.

6. Use violet in all your fantasies!

Violet, the beautiful lightness of being, of playing, of dreaming. The only way out of a black rock and a white-hard place is to imagine all the possibilities before you. Use the dreaminess of violet to play your way on to the stage!

7. Trust indigo and your intuition.

Midnight, moonlight and the depth of indigo. Through the confusion and even the depression, listen to your intuition. Listen to your heart. It knows.

8. Shock the world with pink.
Live out loud. Be you and then some. No pale pink for you! Bold and bright moves you to the center of your life.

9. By all means wear black.
And mourn your losses. Feel the hurt and disappointment. Then clear the way for abundance.

10. Celebrate the radiance of white. The presence of all colors. The fresh color of rebirth and joy. All these colors are present in you. Find them and revel in their gifts.

See, children are all about the black or white, always and never, all or nothing, either-or attitude. If a child fails to get what it wants, he or she feels as if they are just going to die!!! Which of course we adults know is NOT true! But we haven't leveraged the Diva in us to actually act as if we know this! Your divine self knows that life is NOT either-or, all or nothing…so calling on your inner Diva can shift that perspective!

OK, so I hear you…how do you go about adopting this new perspective? First, using the work sheet below, write down every reason you can think of for why you don't have the things in life that you really, really want! A great job, a loving man, a healthy body, a clean house, etc…

Next write down any fears attached to these desires. For example, "I want a great job but I'm afraid to change my current job, or I'm afraid I will fail at something new, or I'm afraid I won't pass the schooling or training needed for this position."

OR another example, "I want a loving man but I have a man now and I'm afraid of being alone, of never finding the ideal man, of being rejected, or hurt."

Get the idea? Good.

Next, identify where you are in all-or-nothing thinking. Underneath every fear, my Divas, is a misconception…a perspective that says, "I know the outcome will be bad." But do you really know this? Couldn't it be just as likely that the outcome will be good? Or even better than you thought?

I am not telling you it will always be good…or bad. Somewhere in the middle is where most of life's choices shake out. Being conscious of this perspective is the first step to adopting a true Diva-like outlook…one that says, "I have a 50-50 chance of getting what I want and those are not bad odds!"

So what are you objections? Don't shout them. I can hear through the divine channels your every resistant thought! Here comes one now…*but what if I don't know what I want? I just seem afraid of change.*

Read on, my divine friends!

EXERCISE

I really, really want…   What I'm afraid of…   My black or white thinking!

"If you don't express yourself, if you don't tell what you want, then you're not gonna get it, and in a way you are chained down by your own inability to express what you want and go after [it]."
- Madonna

Step 2
Turn on Your Diva-vision!

While I have boiled down this to 10 simple steps…there is nothing easy about stepping into your Diva self-if you think you have to rely solely on your own human limitations. Diva, remember, means divine or close to God. And that's what you must ignite, deploy, plug into and rely on if you are to make the next eight steps happen.

Imagine you in the center of your life, in the middle of your own well-written drama. What do you see? Who are you with? What shoes are you wearing? There is no pushing this vision…it must come to you in a still, quiet moment or series of moments. You are moving into discovering your Diva, not creating her. We are endowed with a spirit or divine nature, which is what we need to rediscover here, not invent.

So, before you write this vision down let me give you some guidelines…

Have a clear vision.
Look on stage…get specifics. The clearer the vision the more likely you are to find the Diva in you. A clear vision is an important

step on the road to center stage. Ask yourself again, 'What do I really, really want?'

State your intention.
The play unfolds there on center stage…and you see what it is you really want, ask for it. This request or intention is the powerful and initial shift within yourself toward living the life you want – moving you out of the audience and onto the stage! Taking you to a place between potential and action. With a stated intention you create an electric field of possibility that actually pulls the Diva on stage.

Think big. No! Bigger... like a true Diva!
A great vision is always bigger than your current abilities. If you know exactly how to get to center stage, you need a bigger vision. Growth and excitement come from stretching beyond your limits. Be a Diva – someone who specializes in the impossible!

Expect resistance.
The bigger the vision, the greater the resistance. It is likely just fear of change. Expect it and embrace it. Think of your resistance as the protective part of yourself that is pointing out the risks. Admit and address these risks and keep going.

Expect setbacks.
If your vision is big enough you will inevitably experience setbacks. Accept them as challenges rather than obstacles on the way to creating the life you want!

Get comfortable with success.

We are all afraid of the unknown – yes, even the Divas - even a *positive* unknown, such as your vision. By putting yourself in tomorrow today, you are more accepting of your own success. And you will be less likely to trip yourself up when the vision becomes a reality.

Writing your Diva-vision statement.

Say …. "I am in a theater. I'm looking at center stage and watching my life unfold in a lovely drama, comedy or musical… I am pretending that I am already starring in this production. I am applauding! This play, this life is so wonderful. I love my life!"

The wonderful play is set 3 or 5 or 10 years from now.

Looking at the center stage of your life – who and what do you see? What are you doing? Where are you? Write this down! Post it on the refrigerator and other highly visible locations in your home, office or car! This statement is like recalibrating your desires and goals and the easiest part of making them happen.

If you obey all the rules, you miss all the fun.
If you always do what interests you, at least one
person is pleased.
- Katharine Hepburn

Step 3
Get a Diva-tude!

The extraordinary and unconventional Katharine Hepburn passed away recently at the ripe age of 96. A childhood favorite, I always admired the characters she played in the movies and she wasn't Hollywood's usual idea of beauty and graciousness. She was different…and very different from me. She was tall, graceful, well-spoken and classy. I was short, awkward, intimidated and a struggling adolescent with a crazy family. And yet her divinity spoke to me. She was the picture of independence and confidence.

If you had asked Katharine Hepburn, "Whose life is it anyway?" She would not have hesitated to say, "Why it's my life, of course!" And what was the price she paid for this Diva-like attitude? Well, let's see…she was one of the most acclaimed actors of all-time – no other woman was nominated for or received as many Oscars as Hepburn. She refused any role that was not suited to her and played some of the most memorable characters on the silver screen.

The *Washington Post* described her as "breathtakingly talented," an actress with "unsurpassed durability." She fell in love with an extraordinary man and he loved her back. She had family and friends, many of whom cared for her right up to the day of her death.

So, my sisters, the price for being uncompromisingly you…is greatness.

It's time to adopt a Diva-tude of your own! Whose life *are* you living? Are you living the life you always imagined? Or are you settling for someone else's idea of your life? Look around you…are you chasing your dreams or the dreams others have for you? Are you playing it safe so the man in your life remains comfortable and unthreatened? Are your trade-offs too high? Are you making so many compromises that you feel something is missing in your life. Even if you have a strong and focused pursuit, are you happy with the progress you are making? What is getting in the way?

Many of these answers, like all truth, lie in our subconscious so we need to find a way to get to them easily. I find a written dialogue with ourselves is the most effective way to find the truth about what we want and what stops us. No, I'm not much for journaling, but if you do it, that is great! Let's take that discipline and use it in a different way.

Go Write for the Truth!
(Adapted from the 50-50 Pathwork Training)
A Tool for finding the true answers to your challenges!
(Your writings are for you alone.
No one else need ever see them.)

Writing things down can help you explore your subconscious, your divine center that knows the truth. This exercise can be helpful when things are not going your way, when you don't know what or who is missing, or why you do the things you do, when you feel a conflict between two desires or goals.

In life coaching we know that only you can 'fix' you. Well, actually, we know there is nothing wrong with you in the first place. You are creative, whole and resourceful… You know all the answers. You just need some help finding them…getting through the resistance to go where the answers are… to your center, your heart and soul. The house of your divinity.

To discover what you feel and think underneath the surface, find your fears and where your reaction to them is getting in the way. Again we are looking for where we are in black and white, all or nothing thinking. Try this five-step process:

1. Write down your ideas, thoughts, conflicting feelings, suspicions, etc. No matter how silly, childish, or ridiculous. The more irrational, unreasonable or illogical you are, the more you learn about what goes on in your subconscious. Let your mind jump or wander from one seemingly irrelevant topic to the next.

That's OK. You are on the right path.

2. To start, try asking questions such as the ones we posed in the vision: What do I really want? What would have to be different so I would feel happy and satisfied now? These simple, basic questions and their often equally simple answers or reasons lead directly to your fears and from there to the truth.

3. Don't worry if at first you writings are vague or on a more superficial level - the weather; a friend not greeting you; a vague or small worry. Write them down, all of them. Even though you are working on this superficial level, if you keep writing, the truth will eventually pop up.

4. This may take time and several writing sessions before the material becomes meaningful and revealing. The more you write or put down your random and disorganized thoughts, feelings, reactions on paper, the sooner you can see a pattern emerge about your fears and misconceptions.

5. Do not try to squeeze associations into making sense while involved in this process. The less inhibited and free you are, letting all your emotional reactions flow onto paper with no censorship, the quicker the pattern of truth will appear. It is when we become unreasonable, my Divas, that we find what's really going on and what's really within our power to change.

6. This release, the energy of writing it down, moving feelings and thoughts from body to paper brings with it clarity and relief.

You experience a lightness or ease about your life and your challenges. And in this comes acceptance and the willingness to change!

*There are lots of things that I'd like to be and
nice just doesn't seem good enough*
- Cher

Step 4
Learn to Say NO... It's a Diva's Favorite Word!

YES! NO is a great and powerful word. When we unleash this power we move from doormat to Diva in seconds! But why is this so challenging? Why is it so hard to utter this simple two-letter word?

We don't remember our terrible two's, but we have witnessed it in other children. The two-year-old is asserting her independence. Having just learned to walk a mere year ago and to talk a few minutes ago, she wants to be free from the bondage of the all-powerful parents. The way to do this is to reject their attempts at controlling her. And since she has a limited vocabulary and a simple thought process, her strategy is to say *NO* every time she feels anything is getting in the way of her independence – even as her parents are telling her to be a good girl, go along with what they want and, for God's sake, stop saying *NO*!

Any wonder we have a hard time with *NO*? We are socialized at an early age that to be acceptable is to 'please' those around us and to give in to their requests or risk losing their attention and positive praise. We learn that it is righteous to be accommodating and giving, to value the act of self-denial and sacrifice, and to never hurt anyone's feelings. Of course, our parents were trying to make us good people and keep some order in the household as well. But, again, as a child we don't understand there are times to say *NO* and times to say "the heck with what everybody else wants or is doing." It is a challenge as you mature to see that you can be a good person *and* have a healthy selfishness.

And does this ever keep us afflicted with a chronic case of doormat-itis! We let these beliefs govern our lives. For example, I often thought that I had to give in and please my boyfriends or the relationship would be over. Unconsciously, I believed the relationship was so fragile that if I said *NO* once in a while I would lose his attention and love and, interestingly enough, I was often drawn to people who wanted a people pleaser, so the pattern was reinforced.

There are many reasons we say YES when we want to say NO. We feel flattered that someone thinks we can help. We want to be seen as selfless and giving. We never want to hurt anyone's feelings, so we feel responsible for their reactions should our NO upset them.

EXERCISE: Ten Ways to Say NO.

1. Think of someone you have a difficult time saying NO to.

What beliefs do you have around this? What are you convinced will happen if you say NO? What are you afraid of losing? Where are you in *black and white* thinking about saying NO to this person?

2. Practice thinking of the word NO as an acceptable and honest response to any request. It is not good to say YES and BAD to say NO. Watch and observe when we are in this black and white thinking. There's a misconception here.

3. Make sure to establish in your own mind your right to say NO. Talk this over with someone uninvolved. List the reasons you feel the right answer is NO such as: the person making the request, what is the request, the time it will take, and does it fit in with your priorities.

4. Now, practice saying NO to those most easily refused: the telemarketer on the phone, the clerk when you are returning an item, the perfume lady at the department store who wants to spray you with the latest fragrance, the roaming survey takers at the local mall, the next solicitor to appear at your door.

5. Begin your response with the word NO –get it out there so there's no mistaking your intent and there's NO backing out.

6. Some salespeople believe that you are a YES until you

have said NO three times. So practice saying NO once in each of three sentences such as, "NO, I am not interested in refinancing my mortgage; NO, I do not have time right now to talk, and NO, you may not call me another time. Thanks." Three NO's - Three sentences or less.

7. Use your body and your voice to say NO. Watch your posture – stand up straight and feel rooted to the strength of the earth supporting you. Use a firm and clear voice.

8. Or ask for time to consider the person's request. Then give it some thought. This is a reprieve, not a cop-out! If someone is especially persistent, like your 14-year-old daughter, say, "If you need an answer right now then the answer is NO." It works well most of the time.

9. Now find your difficult-to-refuse friend and say NO, aloud the first time she asks for something. Explain why NO is your answer – and watch her respect for you grow.

10. And, finally, if you want to say YES but feel you don't have the time, energy or money to follow through, offer an alternative that is right for you given your constraints.

As you attend more and more to your own needs and priorities, you are better able to be the giving person you are. And you will give without resentment or anger in a way that is admirable and genuine.

"I have been uncompromising, peppery, intractable, monomaniacal, tactless, volatile, and oft times disagreeable ... I suppose I'm larger than life."
– Bette Davis

Step 5
Tolerate Nothing!

One of the hardest parts of becoming a Diva is reframing how we look at people who do not put up with or tolerate anything less than what they want in their lives. Surely someone this ruthless is not nice, giving or mature and not what we call a Diva!! Let me challenge your beliefs here. What would it be like to go through your house, drive your car, sit at work, be with the family or friends and NOT feel energy drain – slowly, like a small puncture in a high-flying balloon? What if you choose to rid your life of tolerations so you could be the person you are versus the person who puts up with less?

Are we really in control of our lives when we tolerate situations and people who are subconsciously bothersome? While these tolerations are minor – your aunt who always manages to get in a little "dig" about how easy you have it, the co-worker who constantly borrows your pens, the messy office or study, or the car that resembles a landfill on wheels – the time and energy spent dealing with them builds up. These minor "tolerations" build with subtle intensity until you feel exhausted, frustrated and trapped without knowing why. How do you get rid of them? First imagine life without them and then, my friends, *choose* a diva's life for you! One by one, consciously, deliberately, and if need be, ruthlessly, eliminate them from your life.

Getting Started

The first thing I recommend when tackling tolerations is to wear something comfortable but glamorous. Shiny pajamas, a soft sweat suit with a silk boa or your favorite jewelry. This will remind you that you are worth a toleration-free life and that your diva or divinity will help you through the frustrating act of ridding yourself of these pain-in-the-butt nuisances.

Also, if you eventually want to tackle NOT tolerating an uninspiring job, a lackluster lover or friend, or even a bad hair cut, you have to start small and work your way up. Slowly and surely you will begin to expect more and tolerate less. Think of cleaning out the cabinets, the ones you risk serious head injury from falling objects every time you open them, as the beginning of getting the dream job, home or man. And dress accordingly!

A word to those who believe that life is toleration. I can hear your objections…this suggestion of mine is nonsense – there is no such thing as 'not putting up with' anything. There's always something. Yes, there is. I am not suggesting perfection…just progress. I am also saying tolerations are things you cause by your actions or lack of action or your perspective – shift your perspective about things you can't change and change the ones you can and a toleration-free life is possible.

WARNING: THERE ARE RISKS!

There are some risks to living a toleration-free life… you might have to deal with adrenaline withdrawal and the loss of your chicken-without-a-head approach to finding things. You may miss the drama and excitement of having all your energy sucked up by those energy zapping relationships you were hanging on to. You might lose the protection of some handy excuses…like "I can't have people over; my house is always a mess" when the truth is "I don't want to allow people into my life."

Our tolerations are a mirror of what is going on inside us as any Diva knows, get comfortable with the mirror – it can show us so much about our lives. Like a grain of sand in your oyster, says Business and Personal Coach Kimberly Bryant, acknowledgment of a toleration can create a pearl in your life.

As a toleration-free Diva you will:
- Have more energy for improving the quality of your life
- Count your blessings instead of manage your troubles
- Build a better community of easygoing and fulfilling people

Write down your tolerations -EVEN if you don't know how to resolve them.

Make a list and start crossing them off! Organize them into categories. What are you tolerating in your home, car, office, your relationships, yourself? Just putting them on paper encourages the solutions to come.

Don't stop until you've reached the NO TOLERATION ZONE!

*Helpful hint - Notice pivotal tolerations - ones that if handled resolve other tolerations, such as, "if I stopped tolerating not making enough money, I could afford a new car, a housekeeper, and more entertainment options."

For a list of 1000 possible tolerations, visit www.tolerationfree.com/tolerationbank.html

Exercise:

List five things you are tolerating about your work.

These can be large or small including things like not having proper equipment, being in the wrong line of work, hours, pay, commute, co-workers, boss, insecurity, etc.

List five things you are tolerating at home.

Think unorganized closets, broken tiles, faucets, doorbell, location, size, etc.

List five things you are tolerating about your friends, family or community. Not getting along with your significant other, one-way friendships, an outgrown relationship, etc.

Start with these five items and when you cross all these off, start with five more and so on…

"I am simple, complex, generous, selfish, unattractive, beautiful, lazy, and driven."
- Barbra Streisand

Step 6
You Got It All, So Use It All!

This step is simple but not easy (I know I have said this before but truth is truth, right?) It separates the Divas from the doormats. It has everything to do with your self esteem and your confidence. It gets a little heady but hang in here with me…

For most of us the line between Diva and doormat has self-esteem written across it. By self-esteem I mean self-liking, self-value, self-love. These personality traits are lacking in epidemic proportions in the world today. We experience such common feelings as confusion, fearfulness, insecurity, guilt, weakness, doubtfulness, negativity, inadequacy and inferiority and come to the conclusion that we are these feelings…leaving no room for esteem and value for ourselves. Here we go again back to that black and white thinking.

See, we mistakenly think that true self-esteem is the lack of all these feelings, a total absence of them. So we set ourselves up to almost never feel valuable and worthy! This leads to inner conflict, this dualistic all or nothing perspective…which has us saying, "How can I accept and like myself without falling into self-

57

indulgence and self-justification? How can I accept my faults, fears, failings and love and respect myself at the same time? Isn't that condoning them, making excuses for or rationalizing them?"

Yes, my divine sisters, this is a tough one…yet it is at the heart of becoming empowered. Enter your divinity, your diva…with a belief in your ultimate divine or godly abilities you can transcend this limiting perspective – where unpleasant truths and self-acceptance are pitted against each other, turning them into mutually exclusive opposites!

 You can merge this black and white perspective and come out with a more unified approach to this seeming duality. But first let's travel through the dilemma for a more complete look at how this relates to our doormat tendencies.

Some of you 'get this' conflict right away. Others will find this truth in an indirect way. For example, you are insecure and apprehensive about rejection or criticism. You have feelings of inferiority and inadequacy. You have a vague sense of guilt that hides behind other feelings. Perhaps you know you are NOT open to the endless possibilities of living the fulfilled life so you make do or tolerate much less than you could experience. Yes, perhaps you know that you stand back in life and feel vaguely undeserving; seeing your own possibilities negatively. Oh sure, this may be limited to only certain areas of your life…but it holds you back in others. In short, you have some evidence or sense that you do not think much of yourself.

To get through this we need to get specific. What is it that makes me feel so unworthy? What basic belief is behind this unworthiness?

Here is the key – how to face down your undesirable traits WITHOUT losing the sense that you are a valuable human being.

Go back to nature - Like everything in nature, we are designed to change, adapt and reemerge better for the process. One of the constant truths about nature and life and you, is there is an untold possibility for change and expansion. This is our true nature! Once you check in with your divine self, integrate this belief, imprint it on your soul, it changes your despair about yourself. It opens the door to knowing all the existing good about yourself despite your faults.

Unfortunately, unlike a stunning orchid or plump tomato, we resist this natural process. Practice this new perspective until it runs through you like a river…the essence of life is movement… is change and in it lays the hope. When you are stuck you are forgetting that like nature you are fluid! Life and your personality are not static and will not remain that way.

Just considering this view of the changeability of you and nature can help move you forward. If you believe you are unchangeable, you cannot change. Ask yourself, where am I hopeless? Why? Do I believe there is no changing my life? Am I hopeless because I feel I don't deserve a more meaningful life? And am I hopeless about deserving happiness because I hate certain things about myself? Things that I believe are the heart of me? And don't these traits define me, aren't they my true essence?

NO! This is our struggle. We believe, wrongly, that these faults or character defects are us, define and mark us. In short, I believe that what is most offensive to me is ME! And this is the cause for our resistance to change…we fear the loss of our entire selves; we fear we will die, disappear, and cease to exist! Why pray tell would anyone go rushing toward that??? This is why we hold onto our destructive traits. We hold onto them because we genuinely believe this is US…the sum total of US. This is the vicious circle we all know so well.

Now, let's break the circle with reason and faith. You are not your faults. They are fleeting and part of the fluid and moving nature of you and all life forms. Just notice the act of thinking. It is always moving, isn't it? From one thought to another…constantly expanding, taking in new ideas, embracing new realizations bringing you more energy and desire… and a chance at a personality change. These new realizations lie dormant in you, in your divine center, in your diva-self!

It is time to encourage and welcome them into your life.

The Diva is always there.

All you have to do is ask for direction, guidance and faith.

First your beliefs change, then your thinking, then your feelings or reactions follow and then finally you are able to bring new experiences into your life and step quietly and gracefully into your greatness.

In short, you can conceive of yourself as the essence of life…ever changing, fluid and new. You can see yourself as part of nature, gifted with an intuitive divine self with all its incredible powers, possibilities and potential. You know you deserve your own esteem and acceptance. You see the traits you hate and don't lose sight of who you essentially are – a divine expression of goodness.

Exercise: Here's a helpful exercise to reach this truth!

Write down everything you hate about yourself.

Look at the list. Feel into yourself, into the divine center and ask: Do I believe that this is all there is to me? Do I really believe that I must always be these things? Do I believe I have the possibility for love in my life? Do I hold back the divine in me that contains all I need to be completely fulfilled?

Raising these questions, in partnership with the Diva within, gets you more than theoretical answers. You experience a new power in you – one that you need not fear. It's showing you just how much there is in you to love and respect.

"I've been called a diva, queen diva, diva supreme, and I love it."
-Aretha Franklin

Step 7
Security! Guard the Diva!

Guarding the self, with extreme self-care – care that goes beyond just-enough-to-get by – is essential if you are to lead life with your divinity! I was taught to believe that a high-maintenance woman is self-absorbed, less intelligent and downright unworthy! So I was careful to always *look* as if I didn't care about taking care of myself…I was always quick to say how hard I worked, how much I could get done in a short period of time. My value came from self-lessness (or my pretense at it.) I can remember scrambling for an acceptable excuse the first time I told someone I paid a woman to wash my face (a facial) and paint my toes! I made some story up about how I had this gift certificate and just had to use it. Oh, Sisters! Can you hear my pain?

Now that is funny because from an early age I loved the idea of pampering myself regularly. I had a grandmother who I adored, who was the very picture of extreme self-care. She wore only the best suits and make-up. She had her hair and nails done weekly. And, my friends, I cannot even go into the lovely jewelry she wore!

Well, needless to say, for most of my life I ran on empty – no reserves of time, energy or money. I either had a ton or none. Rarely did I think of caring for me regularly so I could build up reserves and be there for my family, friends or myself should some unexpected event need a burst of money or energy.

In the summer of 2000 on our daughter's 11th birthday my husband fell 15 feet off a scaffolding lift. Our family needed me in a way they never needed me before. But I was already suffering from chronic fatigue and exhaustion. I worked too much, spent too much and had no physical or mental energy reserves. This event finally forced me to answer the wake up call that had been ringing off the hook for the prior four years. With no reserves of money or energy but a sizeable bank of sick and vacation time, I literally walked out of my six-figure job and onto the beach – indulging in a 4-day retreat on the shores of Southern California.

When my husband was on the road to recovery, this truth hit me. One-of-a-kind things are rare, valuable and *expensive*… There is only one of me. So I am also rare and valuable and yes at times expensive. And so are you!

So why the reluctance to take care of ourselves? Oh there are a few reasons and we know many them…and we know the excuses as well. But for me I came to see that I was always waiting for the people who 'should' take care of me to rise to the occasion and give me perfect, caring love. And until they did, I wasn't letting them off the hook! See if I did their job for them – that is, taking care of myself, then somehow they got away with NOT taking care of me. And then they would be right and I would be wrong! Yikes! I hate to be wrong. I loved feeling righteously better than those who failed me. Except this doesn't make for a full life. This doesn't make for a Diva's life either.

So taking pride by the spoonful and swallowing it whole, I began to take care of myself. I get plenty of sleep. I have instituted a policy of regular naps. Naps rule. I am always striving to eat better and move more. And I am facing the beliefs that surround my money challenges.

I put these choices first. As the late mega-coach Thomas Leonard said in *The Portable Coach*, BECOME INCREDIBLY SELFISH. WITHOUT YOU, THERE IS NOTHING...

Taking good care of ourselves increases our ability to focus, be productive, and make more money. It give us greater understanding of just how to love and care for ourselves, our family and our friends. In short it 'grows' the Diva in us.

So how do we start the Diva's Guide to Extreme Self-Care? Here are my top ten ways to protect and promote yourself through a regime of self-care.

1. Pampering is good. It does not have to be expensive. It requires time and commitment. Daily, yes, I said EVERY DAY; take care of some part of your physical being - your skin, your face, hair, feet, toes. Take 5-10 minutes and create a ritual for yourself that reminds you how special

and unique you are and how worthy of care. Resist the act of mindlessly washing your face, for example. When my grandmother washed her face and put on her night cream it was like watching Picasso paint! It was deliberate. Attentive. Loving. She looked at her image in the mirror…examining it, understanding its finer points. Not only paying attention to how the world looked at her but how she looked at her world. It was clearly an act of self-love…even in the face of aging!

2. Sitting still is great. I know how profoundly hard this is for so many of you. I too struggle with this, my Divas! But stillness is the only way to relax. To rest without actually sleeping. If you need to make a cup of tea to sit still, so be it. Whatever works. Stretch and breathe, find a soft and comfy space and something beautiful to focus on. Try it for a short period of time and work up to 5 or 10 or 20 minutes! When I first did this I so enjoyed it I thought I would never do anything productive again. Not to worry. I did. And I know recharging the energizer bunny in me and the creative juices that result requires topping off the relaxation tank regularly.

3. Take a walk. Whether you work out three times a week or avoid sweating at all costs, a walk in the neighborhood, woods or around the mall is a great way to take care of yourself. Moving is essential to inspiration and joy! When we move we release feelings and with them the creativity needed to launch our ideas and creative thoughts.

4. Honor the divine. Remember to move from doormat to Diva you must stay connected to your all-knowing, all-powerful center – your divinity! You don't have to be religious to take care of your divinity. You can do any number of things: meditating, yoga, visualizing, participating in meaningful activities that speak to our values and passions. It doesn't matter what – just pick something. Picture your favorite Diva (other than you of course!). What is she doing when she communes with her divine inspiration?

5. Eliminate things you are tolerating which drain our energy and distract you in negative ways. (Re-read Step 5 – Tolerate Nothing!)

6. Spend time nurturing healthy relationships, get the love and support you need from friends, family, co-workers or professionals whenever necessary. It fuels you, fills you - giving you energy and enthusiasm!

7. Learn how to take control of your finances. This is essential for confidence and esteem building and to make sure you are able to pamper yourself, to not skimp on the activities that are so important to you!

8. Stop working so hard. Stop trying to prove your value in an endless cycle of being only as good as your last task! Yes, the managers and employees of the world often want you constantly earning your paycheck and they may lose sight of the fact that you are not at your best when driven to depletion!

9. Ask for help. Yes, you do need help and no, it doesn't make you helpless to ask for help. That is the black and white thinking that gets us stuck! In reality, the ability to see your strengths and weaknesses, to recognize when the strengths of others can help us, makes you very, very powerful!

10. Laugh! It is sad that we have to remember to laugh. But for many of us this is true. I could list study after study on the physiological reasons humor is the "best medicine" but you know how powerful a healing agent laughing until you cry is for us Divas! It instantly shifts your perspective into lightness and joy. It accepts the realities of the human condition in which pain is a given. It connects us to one another in an immediate intimacy that transcends chronology. It releases mood-altering substances into our brains and body and it feels good. Need to remember to laugh? Here's my solution:

Create a laugh list and keep it handy! Choose things that can get you out of your all-or-nothing thinking in a big way; that can lift you up over the mundane aches and pains of life. What's on my list? Well, since you asked:

- The movie *Moonstruck* - all life's challenges told in such a funny way especially if you are Italian!
- The movie *Joe vs. the Volcano* - the truth is so sharp that you can't help but laugh! This is what life is all about – jumping into a live volcano every day.
- The word *flibbertigibbet* which I cannot even spell

but I love saying it! It makes me laugh at my own silliness, scatterbrained and garrulous personality! I can now say that yes, sometimes I am a flibbertigibbet, and laugh!

- My husband Charlie – his friends call him the *master of the visual pun*. Now I am no fan of puns, but he gets such a simple and innocent kick out of these that I laugh despite myself.

- My daughter Charlsie. What did I do for entertainment before she came along? She never fails to make me laugh – and to forget about all the unimportant things I worry about too much.

- My sister Mary Lee - especially when she's debating with her best friend Jim, who is also very funny!

- My father's impersonation of Frankenstein's sidekick Igo.

- The entire book, *I Could Do Anything if Only I Knew What It Was* by Barbara Sher.

- The Marks Brothers. Oldies but goodies.

- The dog puppet from the now defunct Petco.com (*I'll give you 3 dollars*).

- Any and all Seinfeld TV episodes.

I could go on and on. And so could you! Your list will not be like mine and in fact it might be a different list everyday. But just making the list encourages you to laugh and smile and be more at peace with the imperfections of our lives.

"I don't think anyone knows as much about what's right for me as I do."
Mariah Carey

Step 8
You Are the Diva-uthority!

In a recent *In Touch* magazine article, "The 10 Biggest Divas in Hollywood", the subheading reads, "These women know what they want and refuse to settle. Watch Out World!"

Yes, Watch Out World! While we admire and envy these celebrities - their talent, power and money, we are also caught in a conflict. Our not-so-underlying belief is that these women are spoiled, bitchy and downright mean. We say, 'Who do they think they are?' Special? Yes they are special – not more special than us but special because they demand as much as they give when it comes to their work or performances.

What these divas have discovered, and I might add, makes them the very talented people they are, is this: we are the end and be all, the final authority on what is right when it comes to manifesting our center stage. We must lead others to our dreams not the other way around. And we must be accepting of our personal power and authority. Now that's a mouthful!

Many of us have mixed feelings about both power and authority. Perhaps we don't have a true idea of what either one is or we associate something 'bad' or undesirable with them. There's an exercise we can do to discover what our true beliefs are around authority and power. This is in no way intended to blame our parents or caretakers. It is a path of discovery!

Exercise: Below I have divided the page into two columns. One side is labeled MOM and on the other side, DAD. Now if you did not grow up with two parents present start with the one and then use another authority a grandparent, step parent, etc. for the other side. On one side list 10-15 characteristics of that parent, such as cold, reserved, organized, smart, etc. and then do the same for the other parent or authority figure in you life:

MOM	DAD
1. _____	_____
2. _____	_____
3. _____	_____
4. _____	_____
5. _____	_____
6. _____	_____
7. _____	_____
8. _____	_____
9. _____	_____
10. _____	_____
11. _____	_____
12. _____	_____
13. _____	_____

14. _____   _____
15. _____   _____

Look at this list and notice where these people are generally opposites. They won't be total opposites so don't worry about exactness here. Circle those traits where there are obviously opposites. Now ask yourself the following questions:

Who was more fun? Who did you want to be with more?
Who was more emotional? Who solved problems using their feelings? Who used their logic?
Who used reason or logic more?
Who are you most like?
Who had the power in the household?
Who is considered more successful?

When I did this for the first time it was an eye opener! My mom was reasonable, reserved, organized and smart. My father was irrational, warm, less book-smart and given to bursts of volatile yelling and screaming –dealing with life's challenges with his emotions. I am most like my father.

Yet I viewed my mother as having the most power in the household. So as I child I reasoned that emotional, irrational people may be fun (to a point) but the reasonable, smart and holding-it-all in person has the power. Now doesn't this leave me in a predicament? I drew a conclusion as a child that I could not be emotional, irrational and warm and *in* CHARGE. Yet I was more those things than the traits I associated with authority or power. When I thought of stepping into my greatness, into my true and innate sense of power and the authority that comes with it, I often held myself back. UNCONSCIOUSLY fearing if I had the power I would have to deal with the emotional craziness that came with it. And, indeed, I found myself in situations like this over and over again - in the workplace and in relationships. We draw to us people and situations based on our current beliefs. By making them conscious and open we can shift them and then shift the people and places we attract! Yes moving from doormat to diva once again. Your beliefs about power may be just the opposite…but this same insight is the beginning of realigning your beliefs about personal power and authority.

So now I ask, can I be powerful and authoritative about my life without losing essentially who I am - an emotional and sensitive person who isn't always reasonable, organized and book-smart? Can I see these characteristics as resources and assets rather than handicaps or limitations…or things I have to get 'over' to find happiness? Yes. I can. And so can you.

"I don't move on logic. I move on my gut.
And, I have a good gut."
– Oprah

Step 9
Act Spontaneously and Trust Your Gut!

You can't decide to act spontaneously any more than you can decide to be taller. But you can set up things that encourage spontaneity such as stillness, listening, openness, curiosity, a sense of humor, willingness to risk being wrong and to admit it when you are, and trusting you'll be in the right place at the right time and have what you need.

Spontaneity is a response rather than a reaction. ... Spontaneity frees us from the need to over-plan. It puts divine discovery into your life on a moment-by-moment basis.

To be spontaneous is to trust your gut or your intuition. Highly intuitive people move easily between head and gut, synthesizing both together. This is a divine gift that many of us have simply let atrophy in the desire to play it safe. Well, my friends, we are in no need of bubble wrap. We were never intended to make choices or decisions based on staying safe because we are not nearly as fragile as we believe we are. Obviously, this may have been lost along the way.

Exercise:

How do you improve your reliance on your gut? Think with your stomach as well as your head? Here are some ways to start:

1. Listen with your heart as well as your head. Rather than dismiss that first instinct, train yourself to feel the feeling that arises in any situation. This means slowing down! Being still allows you to hear the divine wisdom percolating up from within. We have all had the 'felt sense' – a knowing that we have no words for, a certainty we can't really explain.

2. Listen to your body. According to neurolinguistic experts, decisions are made by first hearing the facts, seeing a picture in our minds, and then feeling the result in our "gut." After you have taken in all the facts and distilled them, move your attention to your body, and after a few deep breaths, ask your body, "What is the best decision here?"

3. Look at the decision objectively. Stand outside yourself and witness your decision-making process. Notice how you feel about having to make the decision in the first place. Do you resent it? Wish it were up to somebody else? Are you fearful of the outcome? Do you view the decision as the ONLY one, right way to go? Acknowledge your reaction to HAVING to make this choice. Let go of the resistance and the fear and get right to the choice at hand.

4. Go with the higher energy. Pretend to make a decision first one way then another. Really get into it. See yourself living out the choice and watch your energy – which choice energizes you? Which one weighs you down?

5. Encourage others around you to go with their gut. Gut level knowledge is hard to articulate, and often needs encouragement. Be patient! This takes time and practice.

"You can't just sit there and wait for people to give you that golden dream. You've got to get out there and make it happen for yourself."
-Diana Ross

Step 10
Use Your Divine Powers!

The way I see it, a true Diva uses three essential super powers that propel her beyond the ordinary.

Super Power #1
Asking for help.
The first is the capacity to be both humble and confident enough to ask for help. While divas may indeed have an independent streak as wide as the canyons of the Southwest, they never hesitate to ask for help. They do not stubbornly assert that they can do it all by themselves! Just think of all the people I had to ask for help to write this book, get it published and to get speaking engagements so I could sell the book! They are too numerous to mention.

What stops you from asking for help? Figure it out. Is it you do not want to be obligated to someone? Afraid we might not be able to say NO the next time they ask us for something? Learn how to say NO and this concern fades away.

Seek first to give… in a conscious and deliberate way (not because you are afraid of saying NO) then you will understand the power of asking for help!

Are you afraid someone might think you are "less than" or "not good enough"? Well, after reading this book you know what you can do with such fears. They are based on a misconception. Asking for help is how great people got great. The not-so-great are still trying to do everything themselves.

Afraid no one can do it as well as you? You are probably right but, hey, you are only one person! And you have a lot of ground to cover if you want to live the Diva life. Let others help even if it isn't perfect. It wouldn't be perfect if you did it either!

Super Power #2
Learn to apologize graciously. To be willing to be wrong and admit it openly. Understand without judgment your strengths and weaknesses and own them out loud! Nothing, I mean nothing is as empowering. So what if someone criticizes you. It is either true or not based on the cold hard truth you already know.

Most of us fear that we aren't as good as we hold ourselves out to be. So when someone 'exposes' our failings, faults or weaknesses, we feel diminished, small, and powerless. We must understand we are not perfect, know what our particular faults are and accept them as the learning tools they are – not ignoring them or pretending we don't have them or mistakenly thinking if we accept them we are condoning them – then we are invincible in the face of criticism or anger.

Super Power #3

Prayer or Spiritual Asking…

No matter how many times we hear this and even experience it, it bears reminding that the surest way to self-empowerment and the freedom it brings is to pray for what you want. And believe you can be happy with or without it. Yes. I know this sounds crazy but we do not always pray for the very circumstances or people that will bring us closer to what we want. So sometimes our prayers are answered in an unexpected way. Be open to this. It is in my experience one of the most delightful aspects of the Divine — whimsy and serendipity and surprises!

What does prayer look and feel like? Well, it is as different as there are people in the universe. It is not always done on one's knees, or using a traditional mantra. Here are just some ways to pray – the Diva way!

Listen to music that lifts your spirit.

Create a space to listen in – turn off your telephone, sit or lie somewhere comfortable, light a candle or two, or close your eyes — then turn on the music. Breathe deeply and slowly as you relax and listen to the music. Let your mind wander inwardly as the music delights your ears and stirs your soul.

Read true-life inspirational stories.

Pick a Diva or two, go to the library and read a book on how they struggled to get where they are today!

Give of yourself.

Spend time loving, playing with, and caring for animals in shelters. Visit your aging parents or residents in a nursing home, be with them and listen to their stories. Offer to baby-sit your frantic neighbor's children so she can have some time alone. Sit in an emergency room, court or other such place and quietly and anonymously pray for someone.

Take a break from the news.

It'll be quieter and you will be calmer.

Enjoy nature at least once a week.

Even if you never put on a hiking boot, see the inside of a tent or the pedal of a bike, take a walk or a ride and look at the trees, grass, sea, snow or mountains. Appreciate the creative nature of the universe and of you.

Create and use a Sacred Box.

Find a box or container of some sort and fill it with items of personal significance. Perhaps photos, a poem or quotes, a comic strip. Have fun selecting items, decorating the box, and finding a safe "home" for it. Then, when you're out of sorts, feeling sad, or have forgotten what you're doing with your life, open your Sacred Box and reacquaint yourself with its contents. Let the energy, and joy you used in creating the chest soothe, replenish, and remind you of the deep spirit within you.

Give thanks for at least one blessing each day.

Do you believe you create everything in your life? Good and bad? Well, if you choose to believe this way you have found the source of all power! See if you can adopt this perspective than you can also consider this: if you created your life and everything in it than you can re-create it! Wow. Talk about divine powers. Talk about the very definition of a Diva.

Divas have discovered that nothing and no one can stop them. They refuse to believe that they do not have the power to change, shape, recreate, or manifest exactly what they need to get what they want. They, my friends, hold themselves ultimately accountable for everything that happens to them.

I am not talking about blaming themselves or anything that involves the self-battering we inflict when we think we've made the wrong choice or a mistake. We will make mistakes. We will fall down and even get hurt. We will always lack perfection! I am talking about expecting setbacks, failures and mistakes and learning from them. Turning these inevitable events into action, using the experience they provide to direct you and give you focus! To take you to new heights of personal stardom in your own life!

"If you send up a weather vane or put your thumb up in the air every time you want to do something different, to find out what people are going to think about it, you're going to limit yourself.
That's a very strange way to live."
— Jessye Norman

About the Author

Merci Miglino has been promoting ideas and people within the New York political scene for nearly 20 years. A former teacher, reporter, communications director, campaign manager, Merci left a six-figure job with the NYS Senate to build a successful practice as a life coach and strategist for individuals and organizations. Her clients include entrepreneurs, career-changers, students, and other coaches.

She is the former Chair of the International Coach Federation's Public Relations Committee and Leader for the Albany, NY Chapter. She is the Membership Chair and Education Coordinator for the Albany NY Metro Chapter of Business Network International. She also conducts workshops for the employee assistance programs of the State University of New York at Albany, NY, the Civil Service Employee Association, Magellan Behavioral Health, the Capital District Employee Assistance Program and NYS Americorps. Merci appears regularly on the local Albany, NY NBC-TV affiliate news with popular anchor Benita Zahn. She has received both local and national electronic and print press including the *Wall Street Journal*.

She conducts her signature From Doormat to Diva© workshop/ presentation for the public through various outlets including adult education, business networks and organizations, and private functions.

Merci lives in Albany, NY with her husband Charlie and daughter Charlsie.

E-mail Merci Miglino at merci@doormattodiva.com to have her speak at your next event, conference or party!

Speaker Info

What do the Civil Service Employees Association, The University at Albany, the Capital District Employees Assistance Program, Magellan Behavioral Health, Seton Health, Vertis Inc. the YMCA, Wireless One, Schenectady Community Action Council, Women's Employment Resource Council, the Knowledge Network and the Business Network International all have in common?

Merci Miglino. Speaker, trainer, coach, and rising radio and TV personality. This short, round spitfire of a woman with a deep New York accent has a heart as big as her personality! Attendees everywhere laugh, cry and fall in love with this extraordinarily honest and caring teacher.

Whether addressing private or public audiences, young or old, affluent or average, men or women, her unique perspective and storytelling is transformational, thought provoking and action-oriented. This dynamo uses music and props to deliver take-home messages that immediately improve the quality of people's lives. With or without power point, 45 minutes or 3 hours, big room or small, Merci guarantees belly laughs, lively spurts of dancing, and moments of quiet reflection.

Merci will come in early, meet and greet attendees and incorporate their stories into her program. She is a speaker who does her homework! Researching, interviewing, and customizing her presentations to provide the most value. An avid learner, Merci keeps up with the latest trends in personal and professional development. In addition to her life and business coaching practice, which includes entrepreneurs, businesspeople, managers, salespeople, career-changers, students, and other coaches, she is former Chair of the International Coach Federation's Public Relations Committee and Leader for the Albany, NY Chapter. She is the Membership Co-Chair and Education Coordinator for the Albany Metro Chapter of Business Network International, past President of the Hackett School PTA and a recent addition to the Hudson Valley Girls Scouts Nominating Committee.

An inspirational humorist and motivator, her many careers have given her a wealth of information and experience. A former teacher, paralegal, reporter, communications director, and campaign manager, Merci left a job with the NYS Senate to build a successful practice. She also appears regularly on the local NBC-TV affiliate news with popular anchor Benita Zahn and with CBS-TV affiliate Channel 6 Weekend anchor Mary Beth Wenger and has received both local and national electronic and print press, including the Wall Street Journal.

Mixing education with entertainment to share insight and inspiration for life and business changing impact! She is a breath of fresh air, a natural born DIVA and most of all a real life example of what's possible for every one of us – a life with purpose and joy!

Merci Miglino
Communications Director
Lewis Mumford Center for Comparative Urban and Regional
Research University at Albany, SUNY
Albany, NY 12222
518-442-2579 fax 518-442-4936
mmiglino@albany.edu
http://www.albany.edu/mumford

Printed in the United States
27838LVS00002B/166-204